TIME'S TIDINGS

Tc

By Carol Ann Duffy

TIME'S TIDINGS

GREETING THE TWENTY-FIRST CENTURY

edited by

Carol Ann Duffy

ANVIL PRESS POETRY

Published in 1999
by Anvil Press Poetry Ltd
Neptune House 70 Royal Hill London SE10 8RF

Selection copyright © Carol Ann Duffy 1999
The acknowledgements on pages 149–154 are an extension
of this copyright page

This book is published with financial assistance
from The Arts Council of England

Designed and set in Ehrhardt by Anvil
Printed and bound in England
by Redwood Books, Trowbridge, Wiltshire

ISBN 0 85646 313 2

A catalogue record for this book
is available from the British Library

Preface

TIME, WROTE Pythagoras, is the soul of the world. It is poets who, for centuries, have experimented with new forms and styles of language to express some aspect of this strange truth. Time is a theme which constantly recurs in poetry; it is an underlying factor in the imagery or the metaphors of poems with quite different subjects. Time is, literally, omnipresent. Since Britain's millennial celebrations are so firmly centred on Greenwich, with all its time associations, it was natural for a Greenwich-based poetry publisher to mark the occasion with an anthology. Peter Jay, my publisher for many happy years, pointed out to me that no anthology had focused on the theme of time in poetry. He invited me to edit such an anthology for Anvil.

Here, then, is *Time's Tidings*: greeting the twenty-first century. I chose to invite fifty contemporary poets, equally split between women and men, younger poets and older poets, poets whom we've been reading for quite some time, poets with time on their side, and poets from a geographical spread around these islands (comprising England, Scotland and Wales, and the whole Irish island). Each poet was asked to nominate their favourite poem by a poet from another time on the subject of time. Their choice would appear after a poem of their own, either suggested by themselves or chosen by me. I hoped that the poets would enjoy this small task and I was delighted by their response. I found their choices both fascinating and entertaining; not only in the way that, say, *Desert Island Discs* is interesting, but because of the curiously catalytic process by which a poet's choice would often reveal something new or concealed about their own work. More than once, two poets nominated the same poem, and I dealt with this problem by allowing a reserve choice. The poem most nominated was Marvell's 'To His Coy Mistress', smartly bagged by Michael Hamburger who requested it first.

If time's subjects are loss and renewal, then time's poet is Shakespeare, the wonderful, true, shining star of our millennium.

He was mentioned in the majority of the correspondence, by fax or phone or letter, that I had concerning the anthology. It was a disappointment to me, although certainly not a surprise, to find so few women selected: a real pleasure, therefore, to report that Emily Dickinson, unpublished in her own time, came second to Shakespeare, before Herrick, Hardy and Hopkins.

It was not hoped or planned to include every famous poem on time in this anthology. Readers may like to join reviewers in playing the omissions game. It may be, for example, that modern poets found T. S. Eliot too close to our own time to suggest a poem by him or a passage from *Four Quartets*. I was surprised to find no request for Dylan Thomas's famed villanelle 'Do not go gentle into that good night'. There was little mention of Yeats. And no Burns! In this spirit, Anvil Press is offering prizes of all its year-2000 publications to the two readers who nominate by April Fool's Day 2000 what in the editor's and publisher's view is the most interesting list of twenty English-language poems not included; and the best list of twenty translated poems. Full details of this competition may be obtained from the publisher.

My warm thanks go to Peter Jay and Kit Yee Wong at Anvil Press, and most especially and affectionately to the living poets here for all their talent and taste and time.

CAROL ANN DUFFY
The Writing School
Manchester Metropolitan University
September 1999

CONTENTS

The Contents is in reverse alphabetical order of the contemporary poets, whose choice immediately follows their own poem

Time's Tidings

AGEISM

I am an old scribe
From a long time,
With a restless mind
And Rastafari eyes.

I am the world you forget
(Or choose to erase),
The one you fear
In your sleep.

I am the memory
That you don't discuss,
Check my kind
I am your future.

I am your place of birth,
I am your good news,
Whose millennium are you?

I am not a star
Just a universe,
I am not just me
Still I am.

I am a way of life
With countless days,
I bring seasons
As I speak.

I am the I you debated
And I created
The hours before your time.

I am an old scribe,
From the first tribe,
Whose millennium are you?

MUTABILITY

The flower that smiles to-day
    To-morrow dies;
All that we wish to stay,
    Tempts and then flies;
What is this world's delight?
Lightning that mocks the night,
Brief even as bright.

Virtue, how frail it is!
    Friendship too rare!
Love, how it sells poor bliss
    For proud despair!
But we, though soon they fall,
Survive their joy and all
Which ours we call.

Whilst skies are blue and bright,
    Whilst flowers are gay,
Whilst eyes that change ere night
    Make glad the day;
Whilst yet the calm hours creep,
Dream thou – and from thy sleep
Then wake to weep.

Hugo Williams

HER NEWS

You paused for a moment and I heard you smoking
on the other end of the line.
I pictured your expression,
one eye screwed shut against the smoke
as you waited for my reaction.
I was waiting for it myself, a list of my own news
gone suddenly cold in my hand.
Supposing my wife found out, what would happen then?
Would I have to leave her and marry you now?

Perhaps it wouldn't be so bad,
starting again with someone new, finding a new place,
pretending the best was yet to come.
It might even be fun,
playing the family man, walking around in the park
full of righteous indignation.
But no, I couldn't go through all that again,
not without my own wife being there,
not without her getting cross about everything.

Perhaps she wouldn't mind about the baby,
then we could buy a house in the country
and all move in together.
That sounded like a better idea.
Now that I'd been caught at last, a wave of relief
swept over me. I was just considering
a shed in the garden with a radio and a day bed,
when I remembered I hadn't seen you for over a year.
'Congratulations,' I said. 'When's it due?'

Louis MacNeice

SOAP SUDS

This brand of soap has the same smell as once in the big
House he visited when he was eight: the walls of the bathroom open
To reveal a lawn where a great yellow ball rolls back through a hoop
To rest at the head of a mallet held in the hands of a child.

And these were the joys of that house: a tower with a telescope;
Two great faded globes, one of the earth, one of the stars;
A stuffed black dog in the hall; a walled garden with bees;
A rabbit warren; a rockery; a vine under glass; the sea.

To which he has now returned. The day of course is fine
And a grown-up voice cries Play! The mallet slowly swings,
Then crack, a great gong booms from the dog-dark hall and the ball
Skims forward through the hoop and then through the next and then

Through hoops where no hoops were and each dissolves in turn
And the grass has grown head-high and an angry voice cries Play!
But the ball is lost and the mallet slipped long since from the hands
Under the running tap that are not the hands of a child.

THE SLOW BREATHERS

The slow breathers,
the saltie in Queensland
the tortoise on the lawn
live longer,

keep the gristly inside bark
of themselves
the less abraded,
the lacy sponge of the lung

in shape, admit errors more rarely –
the granulation under the eyelids
thus slowed down
for instance –

altogether roll more easily
with the regulation roughing-up
from oxygen, that happy, happy
synthesis of long, long ago.

Henry Vaughan

SON-DAYES

Bright shadows of true Rest! some shoots of blisse,
                    Heaven once a week;
The next worlds gladnes prepossest in this;
                    A day to seek;

Eternity in time; the steps by which
We Climb above all ages; Lamps that light
Man through his heap of dark days; and the rich,
And full redemption of the whole weeks flight.

The Pulleys unto headlong man; times bower;
                    The narrow way;
Transplanted Paradise; Gods walking houre;
                    The Cool o'th'day;

The Creatures *Jubile*; Gods parle with dust;
Heaven here; Man on those hills of Myrrh, and flowres;
Angels descending; the Returns of Trust;
A Gleam of glory, after six-days-showres.

The Churches love-feasts; Times Prerogative,
                    And Interest
Deducted from the whole; The Combs, and hive,
                    And home of rest.

The milky way Chalkt out with Suns; a Clue
That guides through erring hours; and in full story
A taste of Heav'n on earth; the pledge, and Cue
Of a full feast; And the Out Courts of glory.

MY DAUGHTER AND RAY DAVIES

She's going out again to that pub in Muswell Hill,
her and that bass-guitarist boyfriend of hers,
and she's wearing those red velvet hipsters.

It's not the 134 she's taking, it's a time-machine.
Look at her hair, it's a disgrace. Mods are gone,
I say, but she smiles. She's on her way to Ray Davies.

I don't know what he sees in the pair of them,
or why he listens to tapes of the boyfriend's band –
him, the writer of 'Lola' and 'You Really Got Me'.

Her room is a Kinks' shrine – all my records
nicked, and pride of place on the wall,
a blown-up photo of the three of them together.

She knows I'd love to come on the bus with them,
go down with Ray (and maybe Dave) to his local,
chat about the 60s, about the bands then,

but even though I'm younger than Ray, it's not on –
might as well try to get into the boyfriend's band,
so I sneak back my Kinks records while she's gone

and play them so loud the neighbours complain,
while she's laughing at Ray's latest jokes,
knocking back the cider to his whisky and beer.

Anonymous

THE TWA CORBIES

As I was walking all alane,
I heard twa corbies making a mane;
The tane unto the t'other say,
'Where sall we gang and dine to-day?'

'In behint yon auld fail dyke,
I wot there lies a new-slain knight;
And nae body kens that he lies there,
But his hawk, his hound, and lady fair.

'His hound is to the hunting gane,
His hawk to fetch the wild-fowl hame,
His lady's ta'en another mate,
So we may make our dinner sweet.

'Ye'll sit on his white hause bane,
And I'll pike out his bonny blue een:
Wi' ae lock o' his gowden hair,
We'll theek our nest when it grows bare.

'Mony a one for him makes mane,
But nane sall ken whare he is gane:
O'er his white banes, when they are bare,
The wind sall blaw for evermair.'

Michèle Roberts

MAGNIFICAT

for Sian, after thirteen years

oh this man
what a meal he made of me
how he chewed and gobbled and sucked

in the end he spat me all out

you arrived on the dot, in the nick
of time, with your red curls flying
I was about to slip down the sink like grease
I nearly collapsed, I almost
wiped myself out like a stain
I called for you, and you came, you voyaged
fierce as a small archangel with swords and breasts
you declared the birth of a new life
in my kitchen there was an annunciation
and I was still, awed by your hair's glory

you commanded me to sing of my redemption

oh my friend, how
you were mother for me, and how
I could let myself lean on you
comfortable as an old cloth, familiar as enamel saucepans
I was a child again, pyjamaed
in winceyette, my hair plaited, and you
listened, you soothed me like cakes and milk
you listened to me for three days, and I poured
it out, I flowed all over you
like wine, like oil, you touched the place where it hurt

at night we slept together in my big bed
your shoulder eased me towards dreams

when we met, I tell you
it was a birthday party, a funeral
it was a holy communion
between women, a Visitation

it was two old she-goats butting
and nuzzling each other in the smelly fold

John Donne

THE GOOD MORROW

I wonder by my troth, what thou, and I
    Did, till we loved? were we not weaned till then,
But sucked on country pleasures, childishly?
    Or snorted we in the seven sleepers' den?
'Twas so; but this, all pleasures fancies be.
If ever any beauty I did see,
Which I desired, and got, 'twas but a dream of thee.

And now good morrow to our waking souls,
    Which watch not one another out of fear;
For love, all love of other sights controls,
    And makes one little room, an every where.
Let sea-discoverers to new worlds have gone,
Let maps to others, worlds on worlds have shown,
Let us possess one world, each hath one, and is one.

My face in thine eye, thine in mine appears,
    And true plain hearts do in the faces rest,
Where can we find two better hemispheres
    Without sharp north, without declining west?
What ever dies, was not mixed equally;
If our two loves be one, or, thou and I
Love so alike, that none do slacken, none can die.

Deryn Rees Jones

CALCIUM

Because I love the very bones of you,
and you are somehow rooted in my bone,
I'll tell you of the seven years

by which the skeleton renews itself,
so that we have a chance to be
a person, now and then, who's

something other than ourselves;
and how the body, if deficient,
will bleed the calcium it needs –

for heart, for liver, spleen –
from bone, which incidentally,
I might add, is not the thorough

structure that you might
suppose, but living tissue which
the doctors say a woman of my age

should nurture mindfully with fruit,
weightbearing exercise, and supplements
to halt the dangers of a fracture when I'm old;

and because I love you I will also tell
how stripped of skin the papery bone
is worthy of inscription, could hold

a detailed record of a navy or a store of grain,
and how, if it's preserved
according to the pharaohs,

wrapped in bandages of coca leaf, tobacco,
it will survive long after all our books,
and even words are weightless;

and perhaps because the heaviness of your head,
the way I love the slow sweet sense of you,
the easiness by which you're stilled,

how the fleshy structures that your skeleton,
your skull maintain, are easily interrogated,
it reminds me how our hands,

clasped for a moment, now, amount
to everything I have; how even your smile
as it breaks me up, has the quality of ice,

the long lines of loneliness
like a lifetime ploughed across a palm,
the permanence of snow.

Pablo Neruda

TONIGHT I CAN WRITE

Tonight I can write the saddest lines.

Write, for example, 'The night is shattered
and the blue stars shiver in the distance.'

The night wind revolves in the sky and sings.

Tonight I can write the saddest lines.
I loved her, and sometimes she loved me too.

Through nights like this one I held her in my arms.
I kissed her again and again under the endless sky.

She loved me, sometimes I loved her too.
How could one not have loved her great still eyes.

Tonight I can write the saddest lines.
To think that I do not have her. To feel that I have lost her.

To hear the immense night, still more immense without her.
And the verse falls to the soul like dew to the pasture.

What does it matter that my love could not keep her.
The night is shattered and she is not with me.

This is all. In the distance someone is singing. In the distance.
My soul is not satisfied that it has lost her.

My sight searches for her as though to go to her.
My heart looks for her, and she is not with me.

The same night whitening the same trees.
We, of that time, are no longer the same.

I no longer love her, that's certain, but how I loved her.
My voice tried to find the wind to touch her hearing.

Another's. She will be another's. Like my kisses before.
Her voice, her bright body. Her infinite eyes.

I no longer love her, that's certain, but maybe I love her.
Love is so short, forgetting is so long.

Because through nights like this one I held her in my arms
my soul is not satisfied that it has lost her.

Though this be the last pain that she makes me suffer
and these the last verses that I write for her.

Translated by W. S. Merwin

Peter Porter

THE OLD ENEMY

God is a Super-Director
who's terribly good at crowd scenes,
but He has only one tense, the present.
Think of pictures –
Florentine or Flemish, with Christ
or a saint – the softnesses of Luke,
skulls of Golgotha, craftsmen's
instruments of torture – everything is go!
Angels are lent for the moment,
villains and devils are buying Hell
on HP, pain is making faces.
In the calmer sort of painting,
serenely kneeling, since they paid for it,
the donor and his family keep the clocking now.
They say, Lord, we know
Lazarus is king in Heaven
but here in Prato it would be death to trade:
the death of God requires a merchant's dignity
and so they tip their ringers in an arch
that runs from Christ's erection
to a *Landsknecht* leaning on his arquebus.
Those centuries were twice the men
that MGM are – God loves music
and architecture, pain and palm trees,
anything to get away from time.

W. H. Auden

IF I COULD TELL YOU

Time will say nothing but I told you so,
Time only knows the price we have to pay;
If I could tell you I would let you know.

If we should weep when clowns put on their show,
If we should stumble when musicians play,
Time will say nothing but I told you so.

There are no fortunes to be told, although,
Because I love you more than I can say,
If I could tell you I would let you know.

The winds must come from somewhere when they blow,
There must be reasons why the leaves decay;
Time will say nothing but I told you so.

Perhaps the roses really want to grow,
The vision seriously intends to stay;
If I could tell you I would let you know.

Suppose the lions all get up and go,
And all the brooks and soldiers run away;
Will Time say nothing but I told you so?
If I could tell you I would let you know.

Alice Oswald

SOLOMON GRUNDY

Born on Monday and a tiny
world-containing grain of light
passed through each eye like heaven through a needle.

And on Tuesday
he screamed for a small ear in which to hide.

He rolled on Wednesday, rolled his whole body
full of immense salt spaces, slowly
from one horizon to the other.

And on Thursday, trembling, crippled,
broke beyond his given strength and crawled.

And on Friday he stood upright.

And on Saturday he tested a footstep
and the sky came down and alit on his shoulder
full of various languages
in which one bird doesn't answer to another.

And on Sunday he dreamed he was flying
and his mind grew gold watching the moon
and he began to speak, with his words singing.

'WHAT IS MAN . . .'

The Book of Job, 7.17–21

What is man, that you make much of him
    and turn your thoughts towards him,

only to punish him morning after morning
    or to test him every hour of the day?

Will you not look away from me for an instant,
    leave me long enough to swallow my spittle?

If I have sinned, what harm can I do you,
    you watcher of the human heart?
    Why have you made me your target?
    Why have I become a burden to you?

Why do you not pardon my offence and take away my guilt?
    For soon I shall lie in the dust of the grave;
    you may seek me, but I shall be no more.

Julie O'Callaghan

THE LONG ROOM GALLERY

Trinity College Dublin

There is nothing to breathe
here in the Gallery
except old years.
The air from today
goes in one lung
and 1783 comes out the other.
As for spirits,
stand perfectly still
and you will feel them
carousing near your ear.
Tourists down below
think they've seen a ghost
when they spot you
floating through bookcases
over their heads.
On a creaky wooden balcony
you tunnel through centuries,
mountains of books
rising into the cumulus.
You could scale a ladder
up the rockface of knowledge
or search the little white slips
stuck in books
for a personal message
from Swift.
Ancient oxygen,
antique dust particles,
petrified wood . . .

Who are you kidding?
You belong down there:
baseball caps, chewing gum, videos.

William Shakespeare

SONNET 12

When I do count the clock that tells the time,
And see the brave day sunk in hideous night;
When I behold the violet past prime,
And sable curls all silvered o'er with white;
When lofty trees I see barren of leaves,
Which erst from heat did canopy the herd,
And summer's green, all girded up in sheaves,
Borne on the bier with white and bristly beard;
Then of thy beauty do I question make,
That thou among the wastes of time must go,
Since sweets and beauties do themselves forsake,
And die as fast as they see others grow;
    And nothing 'gainst Time's scythe can make defence
    Save breed to brave him when he takes thee hence.

Sean O'Brien

REVENANTS

It's four o'clock, an autumn Sunday,
After a hailstorm and just before dark.
The dead are reassembling,
There beneath the dripping trees
Beside the pond, and more arrive
Continually by all the gates.
In the young middle-age of their times,
Demob suits and made-over dresses,
Men with their hands in their pockets
And women inspecting their patience
In compacts, they're waiting
As if there were something to add.

Friends, we are the unimagined
Facts of love and disappointment,
Walking among you with faces
You know you should recognize,
Haunting your deaths with the England
We speak for, which finds you
No home for the moment or ever.
You will know what we mean, as you meant
How you lived, your defeated majority
Handing us on to ourselves.
We are the masters now. The park's
A rainy country, ruining
The shoes you saved to wear to death,
In which we buried you.

A. E. Housman

'TELL ME NOT HERE'

Tell me not here, it needs not saying,
    What tune the enchantress plays
In aftermaths of soft September
    Or under blanching mays,
For she and I were long acquainted
    And I knew all her ways.

On russet floors, by waters idle,
    The pine lets fall its cone;
The cuckoo shouts all day at nothing
    In leafy dells alone;
And traveller's joy beguiles in autumn
    Hearts that have lost their own.

On acres of the seeded grasses
    The changing burnish heaves;
Or marshalled under moons of harvest
    Stand still all night the sheaves;
Or beeches strip in storms for winter
    And stain the wind with leaves.

Possess, as I possessed a season,
    The countries I resign,
Where over elmy plains the highway
    Would mount the hills and shine,
And full of shade the pillared forest
    Would murmur and be mine.

For nature, heartless, witless nature,
    Will neither care nor know

What stranger's feet may find the meadow
    And trespass there and go,
Nor ask amid the dews of morning
    If they are mine or no.

Dorothy Nimmo

BEFORE OR AFTER

I like to get there early when the cleaning
has just been done and you can smell polish.
Or when, in the kitchen, cucumber and radish
march all the way down the salmon and the icing
is perfect. Or before the shop opens when pyramids
of apples and oranges still show no sign of blemish.
When the garden is newly raked, the flowers fresh
and nothing has been said that could be misunderstood.

Or after. When scars of fires and flattened grass
show where the campsite has been abandoned.
When the beds are stripped and the visitors gone.
When the furniture van drives away and the house
echoes like a cathedral. When there is no more traffic.
When everything has gone wrong that is going to go wrong,
all the changes have been rung and weeds begin
to push their way up through the tarmac.

William Shakespeare

SONNET 64

When I have seen by Time's fell hand defaced
The rich proud cost of outworn buried age,
When sometime lofty towers I see down-razed,
And brass eternal slave to mortal rage;
When I have seen the hungry ocean gain
Advantage on the kingdom of the shore,
And the firm soil win of the wat'ry main,
Increasing store with loss and loss with store;
When I have seen such interchange of state,
Or state itself confounded to decay,
Ruin hath taught me thus to ruminate –
That Time will come and take my love away.
    This thought is as a death, which cannot choose
    But weep to have that which it fears to lose.

Grace Nichols

THE DANCE

Painting by Paula Rego; Tate Gallery, London

Even the white-packed sand
darkened by the shadows
of their dance
is rinsed in blue

Blue nimbus too
over the enigma of faces
the cobbled cliff
the small white moon

Moving to a tune
we'll never know
graceful and solid
in the wind's exposure

How they dance –
simple country folk
come down to take a stand
against the blue sea

And time that will erase their epitaph.

Gerard Manley Hopkins

BINSEY POPLARS

felled 1879

My aspens dear, whose airy cages quelled,
Quelled or quenched in leaves the leaping sun,
All felled, felled, are all felled;
   Of a fresh and following folded rank
         Not spared, not one
         That dandled a sandalled
     Shadow that swam or sank
On meadow and river and wind-wandering weed-winding bank.

O if we but knew what we do
       When we delve or hew –
   Hack and rack the growing green!
       Since country is so tender
  To touch, her being só slender,
  That, like this sleek and seeing ball
  But a prick will make no eye at all,
  Where we, even where we mean
        To mend her we end her,
     When we hew or delve:
After-comers cannot guess the beauty been.
  Ten or twelve, only ten or twelve
    Strokes of havoc únselve
      The sweet especial scene,
    Rural scene, a rural scene,
    Sweet especial rural scene.

Paul Muldoon

AS

As naught gives way to aught
and ox-hide gives way to chain-mail
and byrnie gives way to battle-ax
and Cavalier gives way to Roundhead
and Cromwell Road gives way to the Connaught
and *I Am Curious (Yellow)* gives way to *I Am Curious (Blue)*
and barrelhouse gives way to Frank'N'Stein
and a pint of Shelley plain to a pint of India Pale Ale
I give way to you.

As bass gives way to baritone
and hammock gives way to hummock
and Hoboken gives way to Hackensack
and bread gives way to reed-bed
and bald eagle gives way to Theobald Wolfe Tone
and the Undertones give way to Siouxsie Sioux
and Delorean, John, gives way to Deloria, Vine,
and Pierced Nose to Big Stomach
I give way to you.

As vent gives way to Ventry
and the King of the World give way to Finn MacCool
and phone gives way to fax
and send gives way to sned
and Dagenham gives way to Coventry
and Covenanter gives way to caribou
and the caribou gives way to the carbine
and Boulud's cackamamie to the cock-a-leekie of Boole
I give way to you.

45

As transhumance gives way to trance
and shaman gives way to Santa
and butcher's string gives way to vacuum-pack
and the ineffable gives way to the unsaid
and pyx gives way to monstrance
and treasure-aisle gives way to need-blind pew
and Calvin gives way to Calvin Klein
and Town and Country Mice to Hanta
I give way to you.

As Hopi gives way to Navaho
and rug gives way to rag
and *Pax Vobiscum* gives way to Tampax
and Tampa gives way to the water-bed
and *The Water Babies* gives way to *Worstward Ho!*
and crapper gives way to loo
and spruce gives way to pine
and the carpet of pine-needles to the carpetbag
I give way to you.

As gombeen-man gives way to not-for-profit
and soft soap gives way to Lynn C. Doyle
and tick gives way to tack
and Balaam's Ass gives way to Mister Ed
and *Songs of Innocence* gives way to *The Prophet*
and single-prop Bar-B-Q gives way to twin-screw
and The Salt Lick gives way to The County Line
and 'Mending Wall' gives way to 'Build Soil'
I give way to you.

As your hummus gives way to your foul madams
and your coy mistress gives way to 'The Flea'
and flax gives way to W. D. Flackes
and the living give way to the dead
and John Hume gives way to Gerry Adams
and Television gives way to U2

and Lake Constance gives way to the Rhine
and the Rhine to the Zuider Zee
I give way to you.

As dutch treat gives way to french leave
and spanish fly gives way to Viagra
and slick gives way to slack
and the local fuzz give way to the Feds
and Machiavelli gives way to make believe
and *Howards End* gives way to *A Room With A View*
and Wordsworth gives way to 'Woodbine
Willie' and stereo Nagra to quad Niagra
I give way to you.

As cathedral gives way to cavern
and cookie-cutter gives way to cookie
and the rookies give way to the All-Blacks
and the shad give way to the smoke-shed
and the rough-shod give way to the Black Horse avern
that still rings true
despite that 'T' being missing from its sign
where a little nook gives way to a little nookie
when I give way to you.

That *Nanook of the North* should give way to *Man of Aran*
as ling gives way to cod
and cod gives way to kayak
and Camp Moosilauke gives way to Club Med
and catamite gives way to catamaran
and catamaran to aluminum canoe
is symptomatic of a more general decline
whereby a cloud succumbs to a clod
and I give way to you.

For as Monet gives way to Juan Gris
and Juan Gris gives way to Juan Miro

and Metro-Goldwyn-Mayer gives way to Miramax
and the Volta gives way to Travolta, swinging the red-hot lead,
and Saturday Night Fever gives way to Grease
and the Greeks give way to you know who
and the Roman IX gives way to the Arabic 9
and nine gives way, as ever, to zero
I give way to you.

W. B. Yeats

THERE

There all the barrel-hoops are knit,
There all the serpent-tails are bit,
There all the gyres converge in one,
There all the planets drop in the Sun.

THE CUTTY SARK

She has always sailed from
or toward Greenwich.

From or toward
the Prime Meridian of the World –
the zero line of every map,
the hairsbreadth
on the Atlas of the World
where once an Empire blushed vermilion.

She homed on Greenwich
like a bird.

Here
was her landmark.
Here
her milestone –
a signpost chained
through continents and seas.

She stitched an Empire
to her shirt tails.
The hem of lace across her wake
now slips and fades –
her stitch unravels
like a smile.
Our dis-united Kingdom
bumps and yaws.

William Shakespeare

AGE AND YOUTH

from THE PASSIONATE PILGRIM: XII

Crabbed age and youth cannot live together:
Youth is full of pleasance, age is full of care;
Youth like summer morn, age like winter weather;
Youth like summer brave, age like winter bare.
Youth is full of sport, age's breath is short;
    Youth is nimble, age is lame;
Youth is hot and bold, age is weak and cold;
    Youth is wild and age is tame.
Age, I do abhor thee; youth, I do adore thee:
    O my love, my love is young!
Age, I do defy thee. O sweet shepherd, hie thee,
    For methinks thou stays too long.

Edwin Morgan

THE DEMON AT THE WALLS OF TIME

I ran and ran. I was so fresh and fuelled –
The rubble of the plain hardly felt me,
Far less held me back – so filled and flash
With missionary grin and attitude
I almost laughed to find the barrier
As big in its dark burnish as they'd warned.
No top to it that I could see, no holds
Except a filigree of faint worn sculpture.
Is challenge the word or is it not?
Is it the climb of climbs, morning noon and night?
It had better be! What a wersh drag without it –
Life, I mean!
        Up it is then – careful! –
Zigzag but steady, glad to have no scree,
Not glad of useless wings, tremendous downdraught,
Nails not scrabbling – please! – but feeling and following
The life-lines of unreadable inscriptions
Cut by who by how I don't know, go
Is all I know. Beautifully far below
Now is the ground, the old brown beetly ground.
No beetles here! It's the sun and the blue
And the wall that almost everything
Seems rushing to if I dare one more look
Down, there's a sea, a clutch of cities,
Cross-hatch of rolling smoke, is it a war
Somewhere on the hot convex, I'm sure
There's war here on the wall too, written
Never to be lost, lost now, tongues, gods.
You'll not lose me so easily! I'm climbing
Into the evening until I see stars

Beyond what is only rampart rampart rampart
And if I don't I'll take the night too
And a day and a night till my crest like a shadow
(It's not a shadow though!) tops the top of the wall.

I know you can still hear me. Before I vanish:
You must not think I'll not be watching you.
I don't come unstuck. I don't give up.
I'll read the writing on the wall. You'll see.

'HOW SOON HATH TIME'

How soon hath Time the suttle theef of youth
    Stoln on his wing my three and twentith yeer!
    My hasting dayes flie on with full career,
    But my late spring no bud or blossom shew'th.
Perhaps my semblance might deceive the truth,
    That I to manhood am arriv'd so near,
    And inward ripeness doth much less appear,
    That som more timely-happy spirits indu'th.
Yet be it less or more, or soon or slow,
    It shall be still in strictest measure ev'n
    To that same lot, however mean, or high,
Toward which Time leads me, and the will of Heav'n;
    All is, if I have grace to use it so,
    As ever in my great task-Masters eye.

Robert Minhinnick

BOTANY

All I know is, we were there together,
Perhaps for the last time.
The chase ended, and you in red sandals,
Ankles cut by the pipes of the stubble,
And the dog flung down in the restharrow,
A lace of spittle on his tongue.
Below us lay the hot limestone
Of the field's incline, and above,
A magpie's flight blurred like a dice
That rolls unreachably away.

You are still there, with your sunburn
Darker than a ladybird,
And on a pillar of the coconut-smelling gorse
A stonechat, piercing with
Its song the cushions of the air.
Years later I come back
With a camera and crouch down
Under the thorn, pushing the blue
Bead of the lens towards
The orchid that grows in the place where you lay.

'A SLUMBER DID MY SPIRIT SEAL'

A slumber did my spirit seal;
    I had no human fears:
She seemed a thing that could not feel
    The touch of earthly years.

No motion has she now, no force;
    She neither hears nor sees,
Rolled round in earth's diurnal course
    With rocks and stones and trees!

Paula Meehan

FOLKTALE

A young man falls in love with Truth and searches the wide world for her. He finds her in a small house, in a clearing, in a forest. She is old and stooped. He swears himself to her service – to chop wood, to carry water, to collect the root, the stem, the leaf, the flowering top, the seed of each plant she needs for her work.

Years go by. One day the young man wakes up longing for a child. He goes to the old woman and asks to be released from his oath so that he may return to the world. *Certainly*, she says, *but on one condition: you must tell them that I am young and that I am beautiful.*

James Shirley

'THE GLORIES OF OUR BLOOD AND STATE'

from THE CONTENTION OF AJAX AND ULYSSES

The glories of our blood and state
    Are shadows, not substantial things;
There is no armour against fate;
      Death lays his icy hand on kings:
         Sceptre and crown
         Must tumble down,
And in the dust be equal made
With the poor crooked scythe and spade.

Some men with swords may reap the field,
    And plant fresh laurels where they kill:
But their strong nerves at last must yield;
    They tame but one another still:
         Early or late
         They stoop to fate,
And must give up their murmuring breath
When they, pale captives, creep to death.

The garlands wither on your brow;
    Then boast no more your mighty deeds;
Upon Death's purple altar now
    See, where the victor-victim bleeds.
         Your heads must come
         To the cold tomb:
Only the actions of the just
Smell sweet, and blossom in their dust.

Medbh McGuckian

WHAT DOES 'EARLY' MEAN?

Happy house across the road,
My eighteen-inch deep study of you
Is like a chair carried out into the garden
And back again because the grass is wet.

Yet I think winter has ended
Privately in you, and lies in half-sleep,
Or her last sleep, at the foot
Of one of your mirrors – hence
The spring-day smile with which
You smarten up your mouth
Into a retina of new roofs, new thoughts.

None of my doors has slammed
Like that. Every sentence is the same
Old workshop sentence, ending
Rightly or wrongly in the ruins
Of an evening spent in puzzling
Over the meaning of six o'clock or seven:

Or why the house across the road
Has such a moist-day sort of name,
Evoking ships and their wind-blown ways.

'THERE'S BEEN A DEATH . . .'

There's been a Death, in the Opposite House,
As lately as Today –
I know it, by the numb look
Such Houses have – alway –

The Neighbors rustle in and out –
The Doctor – drives away –
A Window opens like a Pod –
Abrupt – mechanically –

Somebody flings a Mattress out –
The Children hurry by –
They wonder if it died – on that –
I used to – when a Boy –

The Minister – goes stiffly in –
As if the House were His –
And He owned all the Mourners – now –
And little Boys – besides –

And then the Milliner – and the Man
Of the Appalling Trade –
To take the measure of the House –
There'll be that Dark Parade –

Of Tassels – and of Coaches – soon –
It's easy as a Sign –
The Intuition of the News –
In just a Country Town –

Thomas McCarthy

A BOWL OF PEAS

for Catherine

A bowl of freshly depodded peas
is overturned and peas go peppering across the floor,
rat-a-tat, rat-a-tat. The dog follows,
sniffing, and flexing his pliable left ear.

One pea escapes from the impressionist sunlight.
A basket on the window is filled with
freshly picked courgettes and tomatoes,
their colour making a polyptych of stained glass.

There is a smell of woodsmoke. It is autumn
again at Glenshelane, in 1975 or '76.
Our shirts are stained with sweat, our hands grown numb
from the breaking of bonfire wood, the antics

of our old Allen scythe. Our adolescent
moments drop from the wheel of sunlight
like a potter's large vase awaiting fulfilment.
Clay is full of love. There is a blob of light

from the future, like a cuckoo-spit on wild grass.
My whole life was preparing itself for you then.
Your parallel life was like a camera made to pass
over me, tracking roundly, taking it all in.

'IS BUAINE . . .'

Is buaine bláth 'ná saoghal,
  Is buaine 'ná daoine meabhair,
Is buaine 'ná meabhair sgríbhinn
  Is buaine 'ná sgríbhinn leabhar.

'MORE LASTING . . .'

More lasting is Fame than the life of men
  For tradition then may keep it young,
But more lasting still is the poet's pen,
  And the book that speaks with undying tongue.

Translated by Douglas Hyde (1860–1949)

Christopher Logue

ACHILLES AND AGAMEMNON MAKE PEACE

from WAR MUSIC

    Achilles went to make amends,
Walking alone beside the broken lace that hung
Over the sea's green fist.

    The sea that is always counting.

Ever since men began in time, time and
Time again they met in parliaments,
Where, in due turn, letting the next man speak,
With mouthfuls of soft air they tried to stop
Themselves from ravening their talking throats;
Hoping enunciated airs would fall
With verisimilitude in different minds,
And bring some concord to those minds; soft air
Between the hatred dying animals
Monotonously bear towards themselves;
Only soft air to underwrite the in-
Built violence of being, to meld it to
Something more civil, rarer than true forgiveness.
No work was lovelier in history;
And nothing failed so often: knowing this
The Army came to hear Achilles say:
'Pax, Agamemnon.' And Agamemnon's: 'Pax'.

Anonymous

THE VIRGIN'S SONG

Sweet was the song the Virgin sung
    When she to Bethlehem was come
And was delivered of her Son,
    That blessed Jesus hath to name.
'Sweet Babe,' quoth she, 'lull-lullaby,
    My Son and eke a Saviour born,
Who hath vouchsafèd from on high
    To visit us that were forlorn.
Lull-lullaby, Sweet Babe,' sang she,
And sweetly rocked him on her knee.

Liz Lochhead

SORTING THROUGH

The moment she died, my mother's dance dresses
turned from the colours they really were
to the colours I imagine them to be.
I can feel the weight of bumptoed silver shoes
swinging from their anklestraps as she swaggers
up the path towards *her* dad, light-headed
from airman's kisses. Here, at what I'll have to learn
to call *my father's house*, yes every
ragbag scrap of duster prints her even more vivid
than an Ilford snapshot on some seafront
in a white cardigan and that exact frock.
Old lipsticks. Liquid stockings.
Labels like *Harella, Gor-ray, Berkertex.*
As I manhandle whole outfits into binbags for Oxfam
every mote in my eye is a utility mark
and this is useful:
the sadness of dispossessed dresses,
the decency of good coats roundshouldered
in the darkness of wardrobes,
the gravitas of lapels,
the invisible danders of skin fizzing off from them
like all that life that will not neatly end.

William Dunbar

from LAMENT FOR THE MAKERS

qwhen he wes sek

I that in heill wes and gladnes,
Am trublit now with gret seiknes,
And feblit with infermitie;
  Timor mortis conturbat me.

Our plesance heir is all vaneglory,
This fals warld is bot transitory,
The flesche is brukle, the Fend is sle;
  Timor mortis conturbat me.

The stait of man dois change and vary,
Now sound, now seik, now blith, now sary,
Now dansand mery, now like to dee;
  Timor mortis conturbat me.

No stait in erd heir standis sickir;
As with the wind wavis the wickir,
Wavis this warldis vanite;
  Timor mortis conturbat me.

On to the ded gois all Estatis,
Princis, Prelotis, and Potestatis,
Baith riche and pur of al degre;
  Timor mortis conturbat me.

He takis the knichtis into feild,
Anarmit under helme and scheild;
Victour he is at all melle;
  Timor mortis conturbat me.

. . .

He takis the campion in the stour,
The capitane closit in the towr,
The lady in bowr full of beute;
    Timor mortis conturbat me.

. . .

Art-magicianis, and astrologgis,
Rethoris, logicianis, and theologgis,
Thame helpis no conclusionis sle;
    Timor mortis conturbat me.

. . .

I se that makaris amang the laif
Playis heir ther pageant, sine gois to graif;
Sparit is nocht ther faculte;
    Timor mortis conturbat me.

. . .

Sen he hes all my brether tane,
He will nocht lat me lif alane,
On forse I man his nixt pray be;
    Timor mortis conturbat me.

Sen for the deid remeid is none,
Best is that we for dede dispone,
Eftir our deid that lif may we;
    Timor mortis conturbat me.

SONG

yi surta
keep trynti avoid it thats
the difficult bitty it

jist
no keep findn yirsell
sitn

wotchn thi telly ur
lookn oot thi windy

that wey yi say
christ a could

go a roll n egg
ur
whuts thi time fuck me

wiv nay
cookn oil nwi need
potatoes

Robert Herrick

CORINNA'S GOING A MAYING

Get up, get up for shame, the Blooming Morne
Upon her wings presents the god unshorne.
    See how *Aurora* throwes her faire
    Fresh-quilted colours through the aire:
    Get up, sweet-Slug-a-bed, and see
    The Dew-bespangling Herbe and Tree.
Each Flower has wept, and bow'd toward the East,
Above an houre since; yet you not drest,
    Nay! not so much as out of bed?
    When all the Birds have Mattens seyd,
    And sung their thankfull Hymnes: 'tis sin,
    Nay, profanation to keep in,
Whenas a thousand Virgins on this day,
Spring, sooner than the Lark, to fetch in May.

Rise; and put on your Foliage, and be seene
To come forth, like the Spring-time, fresh and greene;
    And sweet as *Flora*. Take no care
    For Jewels for your Gowne, or Haire:
    Feare not; the leaves will strew
    Gemms in abundance upon you:
Besides, the childhood of the Day has kept,
Against you come, some *Orient Pearls* unwept:
    Come, and receive them while the light
    Hangs on the Dew-locks of the night:
    And *Titan* on the Eastern hill
    Retires himselfe, or else stands still
Till you come forth. Wash, dresse, be briefe in praying:
Few Beads are best, when once we goe a Maying.

Come, my *Corinna*, come; and comming, marke
How each field turns a street; each street a Parke
    Made green, and trimm'd with trees: see how
    Devotion gives each House a Bough,
    Or Branch: Each Porch, each doore, ere this,
    An Arke a Tabernacle is
Made up of white-thorn neatly enterwove;
As if here were those cooler shades of love.
    Can such delights be in the street,
    And open fields, and we not see't?
    Come, we'll abroad; and let's obay
    The Proclamation made for May:
And sin no more, as we have done, by staying;
But my *Corinna*, come, let's goe a Maying.

There's not a budding Boy, or Girle, this day,
But is got up, and gone to bring in May.
    A deale of Youth, ere this, is come
    Back, and with *White-thorn* laden home.
    Some have dispatcht their Cakes and Creame,
    Before that we have left to dreame:
And some have wept, and woo'd, and plighted Troth,
And chose their Priest, ere we can cast off sloth:
    Many a green-gown has been given;
    Many a kisse, both odde and even:
    Many a glance too has been sent
    From out the eye, Love's Firmament:
Many a jest told of the Keyes betraying
This night, and Locks pickt, yet w'are not a Maying.

Come, let us goe, while we are in our prime;
And take the harmlesse follie of the time.
    We shall grow old apace, and die
    Before we know our liberty.
    Our life is short; and our dayes run
    As fast away as do's the Sunne:

And as a vapour, or a drop of raine
Once lost, can ne'r be found againe:
    So when or you or I are made
    A fable, song, or fleeting shade;
    All love, all liking, all delight
    Lies drown'd with us in endlesse night.
Then while time serves, and we are but decaying;
Come, my *Corinna*, come, let's goe a Maying.

Brendan Kennelly

BEACH SCENE

from CROMWELL

I saw Mum as a child of six playing
On a beach one frolicsome August day.
She was wearing a lemon mini-bikini
And ignored me when I edged her way.
A warm breeze swooned in from the Atlantic,
Bronzed strangers stretched or curled on the sand,
Mum glanced at me. I went up to her quick-
ly and said 'I'm your son, my girl, and
I'd like to introduce myself without
Delay. You're going to spawn me in twenty years.
Let's meet before the coming gets rough.'
Mum looked at me, the old distrust and doubt
Glared into me, piercing my filial tears.
She threw sand at my eyes and hissed 'Piss off!'
If there's one thing I won't do for a six-
Year-old, it's piss off when she orders me.
And yet, because I'm not a man of tricks
Or given to emotional chicanery,
And also since I'm interested in Mum
And her development from nappy-rash
To wholesome couplings with choice lumps of flesh,
I showed no anger but said 'Will you come
Play with me, please, please!'
                That persuaded her.
'O.K.' she said. 'What shall we play?' I asked.
'Computers' she replied 'And robbing banks.
Come on, let's see your knife, your new revolver,
Your balaclava helmet. O sad old man,
Where are your bombs, your dynamite, your tanks?'

Dante Gabriel Rossetti

SUDDEN LIGHT

I have been here before,
　　But when or how I cannot tell:
I know the grass beyond the door,
　　The sweet keen smell,
The sighing sound, the lights around the shore.

You have been mine before, –
　　How long ago I may not know:
But just when at that swallow's soar
　　Your neck turned so,
Some veil did fall, – I knew it all of yore.

Has this been thus before?
　　And shall not thus time's eddying flight
Still with our lives our love restore
　　In death's despite,
And day and night yield one delight once more?

Jackie Kay

THE SHOES OF DEAD COMRADES

On my father's feet are the shoes of dead comrades.
Gifts from the comrades' sad red widows.
My father would never see good shoes go to waste.
Good brown leather, black leather, leather soles.
Doesn't matter if they are a size too big, small.

On my father's feet are the shoes of dead comrades.
The marches they marched against Polaris. UCS.
Everything they ever believed tied up with laces.
A cobbler has replaced the sole, heel.
Brand new, my father says, look, feel.

On my father's feet are the shoes of dead comrades.
These are in good nick. These were pricey.
Italian leather. See that. Lovely.
He always was a classy dresser was Arthur.
Ever see Wullie dance? Wullie was a wonderful waltzer.

On my father's feet are the shoes of dead comrades.
It scares me half to death to consider
that one day it won't be Wullie or Jimmy or Arthur,
that one day someone will wear the shoes of my father,
the brown and black leather of all the dead comrades.

Jean Toomer

SONG OF THE SON

Pour O pour that parting soul in song,
O pour it in the sawdust glow of night,
Into the velvet pine-smoke air to-night,
And let the valley carry it along.
And let the valley carry it along.

O land and soil, red soil and sweet-gum tree,
So scant of grass, so profligate of pines,
Now just before an epoch's sun declines
Thy son, in time, I have returned to thee,
Thy son, I have in time returned to thee.

In time, for though the sun is setting on
A song-lit race of slaves, it has not set;
Though late, O soil, it is not too late yet
To catch thy plaintive soul, leaving, soon gone,
Leaving, to catch thy plaintive soul soon gone.

O Negro slaves, dark purple ripened plums,
Squeezed, and bursting in the pine-wood air,
Passing, before they stripped the old tree bare
One plum was saved for me, one seed becomes

An everlasting song, a singing tree,
Caroling softly souls of slavery,
What they were, and what they are to me,
Caroling softly souls of slavery.

PATIENCE

If I think of my grandmother's house, I think of these:
the black lacquered cabinet of curiosities
that held a Buddha and his temple, intricately carved
in ivory that was yellowing like old teeth, like the keys

when I lifted the lid of the polished, black, upright
piano that no-one ever played, that made a soft, blurred,
tuneless noise, half-felt; of the diminishing black herd
of elephants that patiently crossed the mantelpiece

towards the water-hole on the wall to their right,
and how as they trooped and bellowed, trooped and calved,
what was left of the real herd after forty years,
they bore witness to the skill of ivory-workers . . .

Nelly the elephant, I sang, aged four, close to tears,
packed her trunk and said goodbye to the circus;
off she went with a trumpety-trump, trump –
trump trump, yelling along to the wireless as I pedalled

my tricycle furiously round the floor
under the eye of the black, be-ribboned and be-medalled
grandfather-clock, between the legs of the green baize
table on which my grandmother laid out cards for patience,

running the gauntlet of frowning vague relations
faster and faster, round and round, one eye on the door
but tied it seemed to the settee, prickly old frump,
the trembling, tintinnabulating nest of trays . . .

Was it the boldness of her move that drove me on
and the thought of her all alone that made me want to cry?
For forty years I have been trying to say goodbye
but I did not want them to leave me, and I have not gone.

Gerard Manley Hopkins

SPRING AND FALL

to a young child

Márgarét, áre you gríeving
Over Goldengrove unleaving?
Leáves, líke the things of man, you
With your fresh thoughts care for, can you?
Áh! ás the heart grows older
It will come to such sights colder
By and by, nor spare a sigh
Though worlds of wanwood leafmeal lie;
And yet you wíll weep and know why.
Now no matter, child, the name:
Sórrow's springs áre the same.
Nor mouth had, no nor mind, expressed
What heart heard of, ghost guessed:
It ís the blight man was born for,
It is Margaret you mourn for.

Kathleen Jamie

MEADOWSWEET

*Tradition suggests that certain of the Gaelic
women poets were buried face down.*

So they buried her, and turned home,
a drab psalm
hanging about them like haar,

not knowing the liquid
trickling from her lips
would seek its way down,

and that caught in her slowly
unravelling plait of grey hair
were summer seeds:

meadowsweet, bastard balm,
tokens of honesty, already
beginning their crawl

toward light, so showing her,
when the time came,
how to dig herself out –

to surface and greet them,
mouth young, and full again
of dirt, and spit, and poetry.

Czeslaw Milosz

ENCOUNTER

We were riding through frozen fields in a wagon at dawn.
A red wing rose in the darkness.

And suddenly a hare ran across the road.
One of us pointed to it with his hand.

That was long ago. Today neither of them is alive,
Not the hare, nor the man who made the gesture.

O my love, where are they, where are they going
The flash of a hand, streak of movement, rustle of pebbles.
I ask not out of sorrow, but in wonder.

1936

Translated by the author and Lillian Vallee

Selima Hill

THE ROOM IT WAS MY PRIVILEGE TO COME DOWN ALIVE FROM

The room it was my privilege to come down alive from,
the room I ran upstairs to in the thunderstorm
to where it was impossible to come back down from
without a choir to guide me;
the room where I thought that what I'd found out was
that all I had to do was shut the door,
the room where the bed and the sweets and the door were all
    wrong;
the room in the house like a black plastic sack full of starlings
that smelled of sugared almonds and mahogany,
the room where somebody whispers to somebody else
something they don't understand
that doesn't bear thinking about;
the room where you follow the river
and seal the lips I climb;
the room I want to make absolutely sure of one thing about,
the room where it was like if you go for the door
he'll get you and chop your head off;
where this one thing is the only thing worth living for,
where this one thing's not even worth living for either,
this beautiful city behind the ruby door,
with all its shimmering supplicants and priestesses
and sweets the size of bedrooms
and bedrooms the size of beds,
and little girls in vests like frightened rabbits
too exhausted now to not be good,
is no more than a rabbit-coloured jelly
spiked with splinters of glass that no one sees,
and no one's going to see,

because it's over;
is no more than a deep-frozen household
enjoying the tranquillity of cold.

Anonymous Inuit

THE OLD MAN'S SONG

I have grown old,
I have lived much,
Many things I understand,
But four riddles I cannot solve.
Ha-ya-ya-ya.

The sun's origin,
The moon's nature,
The minds of women,
And why people have so many lice.
Ha-ya-ya-ya.

Translated by Peter Freuchen

Rita Ann Higgins

IT'S ABOUT TIME

One day a car pulled up,
the driver asked me the way to Tuam.

I replied,
'Sir, do you know
that where Tuam was yesterday it no longer is today.'

The following day a car pulled up,
the driver asked me, 'Was there a way to Tuam?'

I replied,
'Sir, do you not know that where Tuam was yesterday
it can no longer be today.'

On the third day a car pulled up,
the driver asked me, 'Where are you today?'

'Sir,' I said,
Today I am in Tuam and it is four minutes to midnight.

'Madam,' said he,
'You've got the right time, but you're in the wrong place.'

Robert Herrick

TO THE VIRGINS, TO MAKE MUCH OF TIME

Gather ye rose-buds while ye may,
    Old Time is still a-flying:
And this same flower that smiles to day,
    To morrow will be dying.

The glorious lamp of heaven, the Sun,
    The higher he's a getting;
The sooner will his race be run,
    And neerer he's to setting.

That age is best, which is the first,
    When youth and blood are warmer;
But being spent, the worse, and worst
    Times, still succeed the former.

Then be not coy, but use your time;
    And while ye may, go marry:
For having lost but once your prime,
    You may for ever tarry.

Adrian Henri

TONIGHT AT NOON

for Charles Mingus and the Clayton Squares

Tonight at noon
Supermarkets will advertise 3p EXTRA on everything
Tonight at noon
Children from happy families will be sent to live in a home
Elephants will tell each other human jokes
America will declare peace on Russia
World War I generals will sell poppies in the streets on
     November 11th
The first daffodils of autumn will appear
When the leaves fall upwards to the trees

Tonight at noon
Pigeons will hunt cats through city backyards
Hitler will tell us to fight on the beaches and on the landing fields
A tunnel full of water will be built under Liverpool
Pigs will be sighted flying in formation over Woolton
and Nelson will not only get his eye back but his arm as well
White Americans will demonstrate for equal rights
in front of the Black House
and the Monster has just created Dr Frankenstein

Girls in bikinis are moonbathing
Folksongs are being sung by real folk
Artgalleries are closed to people over 21
Poets get their poems in the Top 20
Politicians are elected to insane asylums
There's jobs for everyone and nobody wants them

In back alleys everywhere teenage lovers are kissing
in broad daylight
In forgotten graveyards everywhere the dead will quietly
bury the living
and
You will tell me you love me
Tonight at noon

The title for this poem is taken from an LP by Charles Mingus,
'Tonight at Noon', Atlantic 1416

George Gordon, Lord Byron

SO, WE'LL GO NO MORE A ROVING

So, we'll go no more a roving
   So late into the night,
Though the heart be still as loving,
   And the moon be still as bright.

For the sword outwears its sheath,
   And the soul wears out the breast,
And the heart must pause to breathe,
   And love itself have rest.

Though the night was made for loving,
   And the day returns too soon,
Yet we'll go no more a roving
   By the light of the moon.

Michael Hamburger

SPINDLEBERRY SONG

Winter: endure and wait
While frost cleanses the air,
The sky widens with light
Harder, more pure, more clear.

Half-awake your eyes will see
Those only a dream allowed,
Golden-winged swallows fly
Back to the home of the dead.

Fallen leaves, let them stay
Where they stopped, weighed down with rain.
From the season for lying low
Get up again if you can.

But time's the mere measurement
Of motion, mutation in space.
Unbleeding though bare from this plant
Hangs the heart-shaped seed-carapace.

Andrew Marvell

TO HIS COY MISTRESS

Had we but World enough, and Time,
This coyness Lady were no crime.
We would sit down, and think which way
To walk, and pass our long Loves Day.
Thou by the *Indian Ganges* side
Should'st Rubies find: I by the Tide
Of *Humber* would complain. I would
Love you ten years before the Flood:
And you should if you please refuse
Till the Conversion of the *Jews*.
My vegetable Love should grow
Vaster then Empires, and more slow.
An hundred years should go to praise
Thine Eyes, and on thy Forehead Gaze.
Two hundred to adore each Breast:
But thirty thousand to the rest.
An Age at least to every part,
And the last Age should show your Heart.
For Lady you deserve this State;
Nor would I love at lower rate.
  But at my back I alwaies hear
Times winged Charriot hurrying near:
And yonder all before us lye
Desarts of vast Eternity.
Thy Beauty shall no more be found,
Nor, in thy marble Vault, shall sound
My ecchoing Song: then Worms shall try
That long preserv'd Virginity:
And your quaint Honour turn to dust;
And into ashes all my Lust.

The Grave's a fine and private place,
But none I think do there embrace.
    Now therefore, while the youthful hew
Sits on thy skin like morning dew,
And while thy willing Soul transpires
At every pore with instant Fires,
Now let us sport us while we may;
And now, like am'rous birds of prey,
Rather at once our Time devour,
Than languish in his slow-chapt pow'r.
Let us roll all our Strength, and all
Our sweetness, up into one Ball:
And tear our Pleasures with rough strife,
Thorough the Iron gates of Life.
Thus, though we cannot make our Sun
Stand still, yet we will make him run.

Henry Graham

MAL

for Marilyn struggling with cancer

Leaving you early I went through the horses
standing in the silent spring morning
and having forgotten to pee I peed with them
laughing as they looked at me
standing sadly steaming. Your children
were not to know, and so still drunk
the fences and the fields held out
a giggling obstacle, an encore to my
nightly conspiratorial adulterous performance.

Down the hill the estuary of light
was shining space and spiralling birds
as the first bus trundled me back
to where I am today, an ageing
ex-fornicator surrounded by decay
sitting in stunned silence after your call
across the distant exuberant years.

Your father considered me a threat
to your perfect future, in his mind.
His little girl would have the best
not a bearded drunken arty fool
high on poetry and girls' thighs.
So we didn't. What I don't remember.

Now quite alone after your plaintive distant voice
I try to reconcile your dying with my own
tedious cumbersome lumbering towards the dark
and curse the games we play to keep the fear away.

A never-winning race towards own goal.
Then memory takes over right on cue, and all
becomes a silly popular song, it's springtime
the birds are singing and the flowers bright
you're laughing I'm drinking and all's alright.
Outside my grubby window the rain begins to fall
inside my tired mind one word begins to toll.
No. And again No. And again No.

Arthur Rimbaud

BARBARIAN

Long after the days and the seasons, and the creatures and the countries,

The banner of bloody meat over the silk of the seas and the arctic flowers; (they do not exist.)

Recovered from the old fanfares of heroism – which still attack our heart and head – far from the old assassins.

– Oh! the banner of bloody meat over the silk of the seas and the arctic flowers; (they do not exist.)

Ecstasy!

The fires of coals, raining in squalls of frost – Ecstasy! – fires in the rain of the wind of diamonds thrown out by the heart of the earth eternally carbonized for us – O world! –

(Far from the old retreats and the old fires, which can be heard, felt)

Braziers and foam. Music, veerings of gulfs and impact of icicles on the stars.

O Ecstasy, O world, O music! And here, shapes, sweats, heads of hair and eyes, floating. And white tears, boiling – O ecstasy! – and the female voice reaching to the bottom of the volcanoes and the arctic caverns.

The banner . . .

Translated by Oliver Bernard

Roy Fisher

THE HOST

This memory, never mind what it is,
breaks in from nowhere with senses charged

and orders me to move over. Over
me it takes precedence. It's in flood.

Nobody but me has this memory. This
memory has nobody but me.

And for thirty-eight years eight months,
not subject, as I've been, to ageing,

it has lodged in me without ever
communicating with me in any way

I've recognized. There's nobody else
it can have been in touch with in all that while

except through me; and I know it's never tried.
Vampire memory, quietly feeding off me.

William Blake

NURSE'S SONG

When the voices of children are heard on the green
And whisp'rings are in the dale,
The days of my youth rise fresh in my mind,
My face turns green and pale.

Then come home, my children, the sun is gone down,
And the dews of night arise;
Your spring & your day are wasted in play,
And your winter and night in disguise.

Elaine Feinstein

BONDS

There are owls in the garden and a dog barking.
After so many fevers and such loss,
I am holding you in my arms tonight, as if
your whole story were happening at once:
the eager child in lonely evacuation
waking into intelligence and then
manhood when we were first *copains*,
setting up tent in a rainy Cornish field, or
hitchhiking down to Marseilles together.

You were braver than I was and so
at your side I was never afraid, looking for
Dom 99 in the snows of suburban Moscow,
or carrying letters through Hungarian customs,
I learnt to trust your intuitions more than my own,
because you could meet Nobel laureates,
tramps and smugglers with the same confidence,
and your hunches worked, those molecular puzzles,
that filled the house with clay and wire models.

In the bad times, when like poor Tom Bowling,
you felt yourself gone for ever more,
and threw away all you deserved, you asked me
What was it all for? And I had no answer, then
or a long time after that madness;
nor can I now suggest new happiness,
or hope of good fortune, other than
staying alive. But I know that lying at your side
I could enter the dark bed of silence like a bride.

John Donne

A NOCTURNAL UPON S. LUCY'S DAY, BEING THE SHORTEST DAY

'Tis the year's midnight, and it is the day's,
Lucy's, who scarce seven hours herself unmasks,
    The sun is spent, and now his flasks
    Send forth light squibs, no constant rays;
        The world's whole sap is sunk:
The general balm th' hydroptic earth hath drunk,
Whither, as to the bed's-feet, life is shrunk,
Dead and interred; yet all these seem to laugh,
Compared with me, who am their epitaph.

Study me then, you who shall lovers be
At the next world, that is, at the next spring:
    For I am every dead thing,
    In whom love wrought new alchemy.
        For his art did express
A quintessence even from nothingness,
From dull privations, and lean emptiness
He ruined me, and I am re-begot
Of absence, darkness, death; things which are not.

All others, from all things, draw all that's good,
Life, soul, form, spirit, whence they being have;
    I, by love's limbeck, am the grave
    Of all, that's nothing. Oft a flood
        Have we two wept, and so
Drowned the whole world, us two; oft did we grow
To be two chaoses, when we did show
Care to aught else; and often absences
Withdrew our souls, and made us carcases.

But I am by her death (which word wrongs her)
Of the first nothing, the elixir grown;
   Were I a man, that I were one,
    I needs must know; I should prefer,
      If I were any beast,
Some ends, some means; yea plants, yea stones detest,
And love; all, all some properties invest;
If I an ordinary nothing were,
As shadow, a light, and body must be here.

But I am none; nor will my sun renew.
You lovers, for whose sake, the lesser sun
   At this time to the Goat is run
   To fetch new lust, and give it you,
     Enjoy your summer all;
Since she enjoys her long night's festival,
Let me prepare towards her, and let me call
This hour her vigil, and her eve, since this
Both the year's, and the day's deep midnight is.

Vicki Feaver

IRONING

I used to iron everything:
my iron flying over sheets and towels
like a sledge chased by wolves over snow,

the flex twisting and crinking
until the sheath frayed, exposing
wires like nerves. I stood like a horse

with a smoking hoof,
inviting anyone who dared
to lie on my silver-padded board,

to be pressed to the thinness
of dolls cut from paper.
I'd have commandeered a crane

if I could, got the welders at Jarrow
to heat me an iron the size of a tug
to flatten the house.

Then for years I ironed nothing.
I put the iron in a high cupboard.
I converted to crumpledness.

And now I iron again: shaking
dark spots of water onto wrinkled
silk, nosing into sleeves, round

buttons, breathing the sweet heated smell
hot metal draws from newly-washed
cloth, until my blouse dries

to a shining, creaseless blue,
an airy shape with room to push
my arms, breasts, lungs, heart into.

AH! SUN-FLOWER

Ah, Sun-flower! weary of time,
Who countest the steps of the Sun,
Seeking after that sweet golden clime
Where the traveller's journey is done:

Where the Youth pined away with desire,
And the pale Virgin shrouded in snow
Arise from their graves, and aspire
Where my Sun-flower wishes to go.

U. A. Fanthorpe

THE SILENCE

for Jane Grenville

I suppose it was always there, the strangeness.
Once on a patterned floor there was a god
With ears like lobster claws.

And those vast savage roads, stabbing
Like swords into distance. You could see how they
Hated the landscape.

Still there, but other things are taking root;
And still at times, through stripes of sun and shadow,
The stiff dead legions striding back.

Some of it I liked. The big town arch, those
Tall confident letters, the docked words,
Imp. Tit. Caes. Div. Aug.,

And so forth. Nonsense now. And toppled, I daresay.
Nobody goes there. One thing I remember
Of all their words.

A slave told me the yarn: some man, on his way
From losing a kingdom to finding another, gave
A friendly queen his story,

And her people stopped talking, and listened. *Conticuere omnes,*
Something like that. Stuck in my mind, somehow:
They all fell silent.

Nobody goes there now. Once it was full
Of tax-men, and gods, and experts
In this and that,

And the endless stone walls, sneering down,
Keeping out or keeping in? We'll never know.
And their magic unbudgeable mortar.

Strange beyond telling. They did so much,
Then turned their backs and left it. We, of course,
Can't keep it going,

No longer know their ways with central heating,
Water supply, and sewage,
And sickly babies.

They came too near the dark, for all their know-how.
Those curses they scratched widdershins on lead –
Asking for trouble.

We withdrew into the old places, that are easier
To believe in. Once we waited
For someone to come back,

But now it's clear they won't. Here we stand,
Between *Caes. Div. Aug.* and the next lot, expert only
At unspeakable things,

Stranded between history and history, vague in-between people.
What we know will not be handed on.
Conticuere omnes.

CONTICUERE OMNES (*Aeneid* II): Aeneas tells the story of the fall of
Troy and his escape to Queen Dido and her court at Carthage. These words
describe the response of his listeners. They were found scratched on a tile
by excavators at Silchester, in North Hampshire.

'JENNY KISSED ME'

Jenny kissed me when we met,
Jumping from the chair she sat in;
Time, you thief, who love to get
Sweets into your list, put that in:
Say I'm weary, say I'm sad,
Say that health and wealth have missed me,
Say I'm growing old, but add,
Jenny kissed me.

JAUNTY

Light strikes the clock!
I've waited five hours
for you to come
crashing in,
apologising,
kissing my feet,
and jaunty.

Jaunty! I'll give you
jaunty – I've waited
while my mouth dried up –
a wrinkled raisin of fear –

saw the crash
put you in the ambulance
attended the funeral
bawled at the grave
comforted the orphan
collected the insurance –

all these long
clock ticking hours
till you came in,
apologising,
kissing my feet,
and jaunty.

Thomas Hardy

DURING WIND AND RAIN

They sing their dearest songs –
He, she, all of them – yea,
Treble and tenor and bass,
    And one to play;
With the candles mooning each face . . .
    Ah, no; the years O!
How the sick leaves reel down in throngs!

They clear the creeping moss –
Elders and juniors – aye,
Making the pathways neat
    And the garden gay;
And they build a shady seat . . .
    Ah, no; the years, the years;
See, the white storm-birds wing across!

They are blithely breakfasting all –
Men and maidens – yea,
Under the summer tree,
    With a glimpse of the bay,
While pet fowl come to the knee . . .
    Ah, no; the years O!
And the rotten rose is ript from the wall.

They change to a high new house,
He, she, all of them – aye,
Clocks and carpets and chairs
    On the lawn all day,
And brightest things that are theirs . . .
    Ah, no; the years, the years;
Down their carved names the rain-drop ploughs.

PHOENIX PARK VESPERS

I

A man hiking the roads or tramping the streets
Has elegies for hills and epitaphs for houses
But his wife, while she has thought only for the ultimate destination
And is much more strict about weekly attendance at church,
Has much less belief in an afterlife or in heaven –
Thus under the conifers of the Phoenix Park,
Under the exceedingly lonely conifers of the Phoenix Park,
Under their blunt cones and amidst their piercing needles,
I squatted down and wept;
I who have but rarely shed a tear in sorrow.

The hurriedly-emptying October evening skies neither affirmed
    nor denied
A metaphysics of sex
But reflected themselves merely in the fields below
As flocks of kindred groups, courting couples, and footballers,
Old men, and babes, and loving friends,
And youths and maidens gay,
Scattered for homes.

The floor where I crouched was lit up by litters
Of the terracotta cones
And in the darkness at the heart of the wood
Kids played at giants and gnomes.
A woman (of whom I was so fond I actually told her so),
Not as a query but as a rebuke
Said to me: 'What are you thinking?'
And I knew that whatever I said she would add

Half-coyly, mockingly, coaxingly:
'O my dear little *buachaillín*, but it is all one;
Enough of Baudelaire, there *is* no connection.'

II

I think now of her face as of a clock
With the long hand passing over her eyes
But passing over backwards as well as forwards,
To and fro – like a speedometer needle.
And this long hand, where once was her hound-like nose,
At once tells the time and points a warning finger;
Warning me to bear in mind that while the cradle is but a grave
The grave is not a cradle but is for ever.
And while her iron voice clanks tonelessly away
Her face grows blacker under her heaped-over hair;
And I see that all church architecture is but coiffure
And all mystical entrances are through women's faces.
She opens her mouth and I step out onto her ice-pink tongue
To be swallowed up for ever in the womb of time.

TWENTY GOLDEN YEARS AGO

O, the rain, the weary, dreary rain,
    How it plashes on the window sill!
Night, I guess too, must be on the wane,
    Strass and Gass around are grown so still.
Here I sit, with coffee in my cup –
    Ah! 'twas rarely I beheld it flow
In the taverns where I loved to sup
    Twenty golden years ago!

Twenty years ago, alas! – but stay,
    On my life, 'tis half-past twelve o'clock!
After all, the hours *do* slip away –
    Come, here goes to burn another block!
For the night, or morn, is wet and cold,
    And my fire is dwindling rather low: –
I had fire enough, when young and bold,
    Twenty golden years ago!

Dear! I don't feel well at all, somehow:
    Few in Weimar dream how bad I am;
Floods of tears grow common with me now,
    High-Dutch floods, that Reason cannot dam.
Doctors think I'll neither live nor thrive
    If I mope at home so – I don't know –
Am I living *now*? I *was* alive
    Twenty golden years ago!

Wifeless, friendless, flagonless, alone,
    Not quite bookless, though, unless I chuse,
Left with nought to do, except to groan,
    Not a soul to woo, except the Muse –
O! this, this is hard for *me* to bear,
    Me, who whilome lived so much *en haut*,
Me, who broke all hearts like chinaware
    Twenty golden years ago!

P'rhaps 'tis better: – Time's defacing waves
    Long have quenched the radiance of my brow –
They who curse me nightly from their graves
    Scarce could love me were they living now;
But my loneliness hath darker ills –
    Such dun-duns as Conscience, Thought and Co.,
Awful Gorgons! worse than tailors' bills
    Twenty golden years ago!

Did I paint a fifth of what I feel,
    O, how plaintive you would ween I was!
But I won't, albeit I have a deal
    More to wail about than Kerner has!
Kerner's tears are wept for withered flowers,
    Mine for withered hopes; my Scroll of Woe
Dates, alas! from Youth's deserted bowers,
    Twenty golden years ago!

Yet may Deutschland's bardlings flourish long!
    Me, I tweak no beak among them; – hawks
Must not pounce on hawks; besides, in song
    I could once beat all of them by chalks.
Though you find me, as I near my goal,
    Sentimentalising like Rousseau,
O! I had a grand Byronian soul
    Twenty golden years ago!

Tick-tick, tick-tick! – Not a sound save Time's,
    And the windgust, as it drives the rain –
Tortured torturer of reluctant rhymes,
    Go to bed, and rest thine aching brain!
Sleep! – no more the dupe of hopes or schemes;
    Soon thou sleepest where the thistles blow –
Curious anticlimax to thy dreams
    Twenty golden years ago!

Douglas Dunn

THE YEAR'S AFTERNOON

As the moment of leisure grows deeper
I feel myself sink like a slow root
Into the herbaceous lordship of my place.
This is my time, my possessive, opulent
Freedom in free-fall from salaried routines,
Intrusions, the boundaryless tedium.
This is my liberty among trees and grass
When silence is the mind's imperfect ore
And a thought turns and dallies in its space
Unhindered by desire or transactions.
For three hours without history or thirst
Time is my own unpurchased and intimate
Republic of the cool wind and blue sea.
For three hours I shall be my own tutor
In the coastal hedge-school of grass furniture.
Imaginary books fly to my hand
From library trees. They are all I need.
Birdsong is a chirp of meditative silence
Rendered in fluttered boughs, and I am still,
Very still, in philosophical light.
I am all ears in my waterside aviary.
My breath is poised for truth to whisper from
Inner invisibilities and the holiness
Venturesome little birds live with always
In their instinctive comforts. I am shedding
The appetites of small poetry and open to
Whatever visits me. I am all eyes
When light moves on water and the leaves shake.
I am very still, a hedge-hidden sniper
In whose sights clarified infinity sits

Smiling at me, and my skin is alive
To thousands of brushed touches, very light
Delicate kisses of time, thought kisses,
Touches which have come out of hiding shyly
Then go back again into the far away
Surrender they came from and where they live.
Perfecting my afternoon, I am alert to
Archival fragrances that float to me
Unexplained over the world's distances.
This is my time. I am making it real.
I am getting rid of myself. This is my time.
I am free to do whatever I wish
In these hours, and I have chosen this
Liberty, which is an evanishment
To the edges of breath, a momentary
Loss of the dutiful, a destitute
Perchance, a slipping away from life's
Indignities and works into my freedom
Which is beyond all others and is me.
I am free to do as I like, and do this;
I sink like a slow root in the name of life
And in the name of what it is I do.
These are my hours of 1993.
Ears, eyes, nose, skin and taste have gone.
For a little while I shall be nothing and good.
Then other time will come back, and history.
I shall get up and leave my hiding place,
My instinctive, field-sized republic.
I shall go home, and be that other man.
I shall go to my office. I shall live
Another year longing for my hours
In the complete afternoon of sun and salt.
My empty shoes at the bedside will say to me,
'When are we taking you back? Why be patient?
You have much more, so much more, to lose.'

William Shakespeare

from MACBETH: ACT V, SCENE 5

Tomorrow, and tomorrow, and tomorrow,
Creeps in this petty pace from day to day
To the last syllable of recorded time;
And all our yesterdays have lighted fools
The way to dusty death. Out, out, brief candle!
Life's but a walking shadow, a poor player
That struts and frets his hour upon the stage
And then is heard no more. It is a tale
Told by an idiot, full of sound and fury,
Signifying nothing.

Carol Ann Duffy

DEMETER

Where I lived – winter and hard earth.
I sat in my cold stone room
choosing tough words, granite, flint,

to break the ice. My broken heart –
I tried that, but it skimmed,
flat, over the frozen lake.

She came from a long, long way,
but I saw her at last, walking,
my daughter, my girl, across the fields,

in bare feet, bringing all spring's flowers
to her mother's house. I swear
the air softened and warmed as she moved,

the blue sky smiling, none too soon,
with the small shy mouth of a new moon.

DONAL OG

It is late last night the dog was speaking of you;
the snipe was speaking of you in her deep marsh.
It is you are the lonely bird through the woods;
and that you may be without a mate until you find me.

You promised me, and you said a lie to me,
that you would be before me where the sheep are flocked;
I gave a whistle and three hundred cries to you,
and I found nothing there but a bleating lamb.

You promised me a thing that was hard for you,
a ship of gold under a silver mast;
twelve towns with a market in all of them,
and a fine white court by the side of the sea.

You promised me a thing that is not possible,
that you would give me gloves of the skin of a fish;
that you would give me shoes of the skin of a bird;
and a suit of the dearest silk in Ireland.

When I go by myself to the Well of Loneliness,
I sit down and I go through my trouble;
when I see the world and do not see my boy,
he that has an amber shade in his hair.

It was on that Sunday I gave my love to you;
the Sunday that is last before Easter Sunday.
And myself on my knees reading the Passion;
and my two eyes giving love to you for ever.

My mother said to me not to be talking with you today,
or tomorrow, or on the Sunday;
it was a bad time she took for telling me that;
it was shutting the door after the house was robbed.

My heart is as black as the blackness of the sloe,
or as the black coal that is on the smith's forge;
or as the sole of a shoe left in white halls;
it was you put that darkness over my life.

You have taken the east from me; you have taken the west from me;
you have taken what is before me and what is behind me;
you have taken the moon, you have taken the sun from me;
and my fear is great that you have taken God from me!

Translated by Lady Augusta Gregory (1852–1932)

Gillian Clarke

THE STONE HARE

Think of it waiting three hundred million years,
not a hare hiding in the last stand of wheat,
but a premonition of stone, a moonlit reef
where corals reach for the light through clear

waters of warm Palaeozoic seas.
In its limbs lie the story of the earth,
the living ocean, then the slow birth
of limestone from the long trajectories

of starfish, feather-stars, crinoids and crushed shells
that fill with calcite, harden, wait for the quarryman,
the timed explosion and the sculptor's hand.
Then the hare, its eye a planet, springs from the chisel

to stand in the grass, moonlight's muscle and bone,
the stems of sea-lilies slowly turned to stone.

Alun Lewis

IN HOSPITAL: POONA (1)

Last night I did not fight for sleep
But lay awake from midnight while the world
Turned its slow features to the moving deep
Of darkness, till I knew that you were furled,

Beloved, in the same dark watch as I.
And sixty degrees of longitude beside
Vanished as though a swan in ecstasy
Had spanned the distance from your sleeping side.

And like to swan or moon the whole of Wales
Glided within the parish of my care:
I saw the green tide leap on Cardigan,
Your red yacht riding like a legend there,

And the great mountains, Dafydd and Llewelyn,
Plynlimmon, Cader Idris and Eryri
Threshing the darkness back from head and fin,
And also the small nameless mining valley

Whose slopes are scratched with streets and sprawling graves
Dark in the lap of firwoods and great boulders
Where you lay waiting, listening to the waves –
My hot hands touched your white despondent shoulders

– And then ten thousand miles of daylight grew
Between us, and I heard the wild daws crake
In India's starving throat; whereat I knew
That Time upon the heart can break
But love survives the venom of the snake.

Kate Clanchy

WHEN MY GRANDMOTHER SAID SHE SHOULD NEVER HAVE LEFT

New Zealand, land of her birth,
breakfast lamb-chops,
and frequent, casual earthquakes –
it frightened us.
To cast her net so very wide
over years, decades, lives –
was like a ground tremor starting,
spreading quick as misgivings,
wrinkling oceans, rumpling borders,
spiralling out of the Southern hemisphere
to compass Moscow and the War,
lap at England, Hampshire, here.

And then to let the sonar rings
reach our feet and pass us,
loop us, to pull them back
with that single gesture,
uptailing me, my cousins, brother,
into new volcanic fissures,
dowsing my father, uncle, aunt
in the China Sea till they paled to thoughts;
letting all our books and paintings
bob to other hands, like jetsam,
to push even my grandfather under
with his Captain's hat, his careful letters;

to furl all this in her fist at the epicentre,
where she stood, fifteen,
a skinny, straight-browed girl,

waiting for plates to settle flat
on the dresser, her cup
to click in the dent in the saucer,
the framed map of the Empire
to sway back horizontal,
for everything to be
as if nothing had happened,
and then to toss the twisted paper
in the grate to light a fire, later –

that shook me.

Robert Browning

MEMORABILIA

Ah, did you once see Shelley plain,
    And did he stop and speak to you,
And did you speak to him again?
    How strange it seems and new!

But you were living before that,
    And also you are living after,
And the memory I started at –
    My starting moves your laughter.

I crossed a moor, with a name of its own
    And a certain use in the world no doubt,
Yet a hand's-breadth of it shines alone
    'Mid the blank miles round about:

For there I picked up on the heather
    And there I put inside my breast
A moulted feather, an eagle-feather!
    Well, I forget the rest.

Charles Causley

EDEN ROCK

They are waiting for me somewhere beyond Eden Rock:
My father, twenty-five, in the same suit
Of Genuine Irish Tweed, his terrier Jack
Still two years old and trembling at his feet.

My mother, twenty-three, in a sprigged dress
Drawn at the waist, ribbon in her straw hat,
Has spread the stiff white cloth over the grass.
Her hair, the colour of wheat, takes on the light.

She pours tea from a Thermos, the milk straight
From an old H.P. sauce bottle, a screw
Of paper for a cork; slowly sets out
The same three plates, the tin cups painted blue.

The sky whitens as if lit by three suns.
My mother shades her eyes and looks my way
Over the drifted stream. My father spins
A stone along the water. Leisurely,

They beckon to me from the other bank.
I hear them call, 'See where the stream-path is!
Crossing is not as hard as you might think.'

I had not thought that it would be like this.

Frances Bellerby

ENDS MEET

My grandmother came down the steps into the garden.
She shone in the gauzy air.
She said: 'There's an old woman at the gate –
See what she wants, my dear.'

My grandmother's eyes were blue like the damsels
Darting and swerving above the stream,
Or like the kingfisher arrow shot into darkness
Through the archway's dripping gleam.

My grandmother's hair was silver as sunlight.
The sun had been poured right over her, I saw,
And ran down her dress and spread a pool for her shadow
To float in. And she would live for evermore.

There was nobody at the gate when I got there.
Not even a shadow hauling along the road,
Nor my yellow snail delicate under the ivy,
Nor my sheltering cold-stone toad.

But the sunflowers aloft were calm. They'd seen no one.
They were sucking light, for ever and a day.
So I busied myself with going away unheeded
And with having nothing to say.

No comment, nothing to tell, or to think,
Whilst the day followed the homing sun.
There was no old woman at my grandmother's gate.

And there isn't at mine.

POSTMERIDIAN

1

After the morning has cut the sediment of night
with luminous acids, here is the afternoon
slowly recovering, getting heavier,
feeding on the general tiredness.
Here is the afternoon with its look
of a middle-aged woman who once
committed a crime, long ago,
never discovered, forgotten, of no consequence;
she now passes, always unnoticed.
Most people sleep, or feel, even
while still at work, their gestures slow motion.
The afternoon passes among them, through them,
moving its heavy haunches.

2

The great rest, the great parties, the great solitudes
take place at night, when one possesses time,
when, after work, time finds itself
in the man in the North Railway Station,
in the woman in the South Railway Station,
in the deaf-mutes in the restaurant,
whose quiet liveliness does not contaminate anyone,
in a certain nuptial room,
in a certain attitude of sleep,
in a particular dream in the shape of a rhombus.

3

The afternoon is intermediary time.
Those who love lack the courage to show themselves.
Those who are loved let themselves be waited for.
Waiting expands chairs,
flattens the telephone,
the walls become pneumatic;
you hit your head against them in vain; it doesn't hurt –
the entire universe is anaesthetized.

Those who love ring the doorbell, and when you open
there is nobody there; somebody ran away leaving behind
a delicate ectoplasm which disappears
if you breathe too heavily.
And so, between those who left and those who did not come,
you stand frozen, disfigured,
tattooed on the air.

4

In the afternoon, the cobras sleep.
In their long slumber only the venom stays awake,
like a violet light bulb.
The lions with their wise jaws sleep.
In the sky, the pale soul of the stars.
In the alphabet, the letter 'M', the letter 'N',
closely embraced, sleep.

5

Postmeridian – take care:
day is half gone; you've already forgotten
the sparkling thorns of sunrise;

the speed of light in the tree's spine
now has passed its peak.
After the cold waters of dawn sculpted you,
experience was deposited on your body
in thin layers, invisible.

6

If you could live
the tea hours, the coffee hours,
the tranquil sound of cups,
if you could conceive of the fragile amber hours,
the afternoon of an old family in an old century
altered by a romantic memory,
if only you would resist the horror
of seeing your face in the cupful
of tea, burning in the flames of Hell.

Or, in the later afternoon hours,
have you ever seen the sudden rain of wrinkles
falling on your visitor's cheek?
It is as if the light's decline
would first test its victim,
then abandon it without going for the kill,
leaving it terrorized for the rest of its life.
And you who watch say nothing,
only ask yourself if the same mass of wrinkles,
like a living creature, didn't throb for an instant
on your own face. You do something, anything –
for example, light a cigarette –
and, finally, twilight saves you.

Finally, the air is cool, like the body after love.
The vapors of premonition are lost.
The afternoon moves to the other side of the globe,
with its aspect of a middle-aged woman,

each hand carrying a loaded shopping bag.
Who knows what they contain? Maybe flour, maybe raw meat.
In any case, some bloody streaks were observed in her wake,
in the railway station, in the lion's eye,
in the cup of tea. Don't worry about it now.
From the newspapers, tomorrow,
we'll find out what really happened.

Translated by Cristian Andrei, Naomi Lazard and Nina Cassian

William Wordsworth

MUTABILITY

From low to high doth dissolution climb,
And sink from high to low, along a scale
Of awful notes, whose concord shall not fail;
A musical but melancholy chime,
Which they can hear who meddle not with crime,
Nor avarice, nor over-anxious care.
Truth fails not; but her outward forms that bear
The longest date do melt like frosty rime,
That in the morning whitened hill and plain
And is no more; drop like the tower sublime
Of yesterday, which royally did wear
His crown of weeds, but could not even sustain
Some casual shout that broke the silent air,
Or the unimaginable touch of Time.

DE

De snow, de sleet, de lack o'heat,
De wishy-washy sunlight,
De lip turn blue, de cold, 'ACHOO!'
De runny nose, de frostbite,

De creakin' knee, de misery,
De joint dem all rheumatic,
De icy bed, (de blanket dead)
De burs' pipe in de attic.

De window a-shake, de glass near break,
De wind dat cut like razor,
De wonderin' why you never buy
De window from dat double-glazer.

De heavy coat, zip to de throat,
De nose an' ears all pinky,
De weepin' sky, de clothes can't dry,
De day dem long an' inky.

De icy road, de heavy load,
De las' minute Christmus shoppin'
De cuss an' fret 'cause you feget
De ribbon an' de wrappin'.

De mud, de grime, de slush, de slime,
De place gloomy since November,
De sinkin' heart, is jus' de start, o'
De wintertime,
December.

THE NEGRO SPEAKS OF RIVERS

I've known rivers:
I've known rivers ancient as the world and older than the flow of
    human blood in human veins.

My soul has grown deep like the rivers.

I bathed in the Euphrates when dawns were young.
I built my hut near the Congo and it lulled me to sleep.

I looked upon the Nile and raised the pyramids above it.
I heard the singing of the Mississippi when Abe Lincoln went
    down to New Orleans, and I've seen its muddy bosom turn
    all golden in the sunset.

I've known rivers:
Ancient, dusky rivers.

My soul has grown deep like the rivers.

Sujata Bhatt

SRUTI

> *Sruti means 'to hear' or 'that which is heard'.*
> *Musically it points to the interval between notes*
> *which can be just perceived auditorily.*
>
> — B. C. DEVA

You, who first said *sruti*,
what did you hear?

Between the sound of your footsteps
and the cry of a bird by the river
did you hear another?
Did you continue walking?

Where did you turn
to measure your scale?

Between the sound of a horse
stepping forward: his bare skin quivering, his head raised,
and the sound of a woman
buying rice, didn't you hear another
and yet another sound?

What did you listen for
to count your notes?

You, who first said *sruti*,
you keep me sleepless.
I'm trying to find a way
to return to the world that you once heard.

'BECAUSE I COULD NOT STOP FOR DEATH'

Because I could not stop for Death –
He kindly stopped for me –
The Carriage held but just Ourselves –
And Immortality.

We slowly drove – He knew no haste
And I had put away
My labor and my leisure too,
For His Civility –

We passed the School, where Children strove
At Recess – in the Ring –
We passed the Fields of Gazing Grain –
We passed the Setting Sun –

Or rather – He passed Us –
The Dews drew quivering and chill –
For only Gossamer, my Gown –
My Tippet – only Tulle –

We paused before a House that seemed
A Swelling of the Ground –
The Roof was scarcely visible –
The Cornice – in the Ground –

Since then – 'tis Centuries – and yet
Feels shorter than the Day
I first surmised the Horses' Heads
Were toward Eternity –

Simon Armitage

TWO CLOCKS

In the same bedroom we kept two small clocks,
one you could set your watch by, the other

you could not. The night we lost the good clock
under the bed, the other seemed to know

to take its turn, and was a metronome
until the lost clock was found. Then it stopped.

Like emergency lighting kicking in
during a power-cut, or biking it

half asleep on the back of a tandem,
or gliding home with the engine broken.

And since neither of us can talk freely
on Albert Einstein's General Theory,

electromagnetic flux, black magic
or the paranormal, let us imagine

that all objects and events are open
to any meaning we choose to give them,

and that if the absence of one timepiece
causes another to take up the pace,

then these clocks could be said to demonstrate
some aspect of our love or private thoughts.

Stretching the point to another level,
maybe the effect is causal, and life –

if we could get things right on a small scale,
between people – might conform to this rule

of like for like – it could be that simple.
Maybe these clocks are a poor example.

D. H. Lawrence

NEW YEAR'S NIGHT

Now you are mine, to-night at last I say it;
You're a dove I have bought for sacrifice,
And to-night I slay it.

Here in my arms my naked sacrifice!
Death, do you hear, in my arms I am bringing
My offering, bought at great price.

She's a silvery dove worth more than all I've got.
Now I offer her up to the ancient, inexorable God,
Who knows me not.

Look, she's a wonderful dove, without blemish or spot!
I sacrifice all in her, my last of the world,
Pride, strength, all the lot.

All, all on the altar! And death swooping down
Like a falcon. 'Tis God has taken the victim;
I have won my renown.

Moniza Alvi

MY FATHER'S FATHER'S FATHER

In this city I have aged thousands of years.
I am older than the oldest tree in the world.

There are homes here for ancient holy cows
but none for old people, nowhere for me to go.

It is good that like the cows I am prepared
to wander the lanes and alleyways.

I was here before my father's father's father –
I think I can identify him, rising upwards

like K2 on an early relief map of India.
He is so old his skin is flaking like leaves,

his hair is soft as dust. I take his arm,
tell him who I am, then we are old together.

We vow to bathe ourselves everyday although
we are so old, because like the city

we are hanging by a tough thread
and dead-looking trees

have brilliant purple flowers.

Rabindranath Tagore

REMEMBERING

I don't remember my mother.
    Only this: sometimes when I'm at play,
        suddenly, for no reason at all,
a tune begins to buzz
        and ring in my ears,
and my mother comes
        and merges with my play.
Maybe she used to sing,
        rocking me.
She has gone
        and left her song behind.

I don't remember my mother.
    Only this: when in Ashwin
        at dawn among shiuli trees
the scent of their flowers
        is borne by the dewy breeze,
somehow then she comes back to my mind –
        my mother.
Long ago perhaps she gathered shiulis,
        filling her basket.
So the scent of Puja
        returns as her scent.

I don't remember my mother.
    Only this: when I sit by the window
of my bedroom
        and look at the far blue sky,
it seems to me my mother's looking at me
        with steady eyes.

Long ago she used to hold me on her lap
      and look at my face.
That's the look she has left
      in all the sky.

Translated by Ketaki Kushari Dyson

John Agard

HOW LAUGHTER MADE CLOCK SMILE

To make Clock smile
even a little smile.
That's what Laughter wanted to do.

So Laughter stared at Clock
Clock didn't.

Laughter clapped hands
Clock didn't.

Laughter made a funny face
Clock didn't.

Laughter asked Clock
have you any idea of the time?

Clock chuckled.

Alexander Pushkin

LINES WRITTEN AT NIGHT DURING INSOMNIA

I can't sleep; no light burns;
All round, darkness, irksome sleep.
Only the monotonous
Ticking of the clock,
The old wives' chatter of fate,
Trembling of the sleeping night,
Mouse-like scurrying of life . . .
Why do you disturb me?
What do you mean, tedious whispers?
Is it the day I have wasted
Reproaching me or murmuring?
What do you want from me?
Are you calling me or prophesying?
I want to understand you,
I seek a meaning in you . . .

Translated by D. M. Thomas

Fleur Adcock

FOR A FIVE-YEAR-OLD

A snail is climbing up the window-sill
Into your room, after a night of rain.
You call me in to see, and I explain
That it would be unkind to leave it there:
It might crawl to the floor; we must take care
That no one squashes it. You understand,
And carry it outside, with careful hand,
To eat a daffodil.

I see, then, that a kind of faith prevails:
Your gentleness is moulded still by words
From me, who have trapped mice and shot wild birds,
From me, who drowned your kittens, who betrayed
Your closest relatives, and who purveyed
The harshest kind of truth to many another.
But that is how things are: I am your mother,
And we are kind to snails.

Sir Walter Raleigh

'EVEN SUCH IS TIME . . .'

Even such is Time, which takes in trust
Our youth, our joys, and all we have,
And pays us but with age and dust;
Who, in the dark and silent grave,
When we have wandered all our ways,
Shuts up the story of our days.
But from this earth, this grave, this dust,
The Lord shall raise me up, I trust.

Dannie Abse

PHOTOGRAPH AND WHITE TULIPS

A little nearer please. And a little nearer
we move to the window, to the polished table.
Objects become professional: mannequins
preening themselves before an audience. Only
the tulips, self-absorbed, ignore the camera.

All photographs flatter us if we wait
long enough. So we awkwardly Smile please
while long-necked tulips, sinuous out of the vase,
droop over the polished table. They're entranced
by their own puffed and smudgy reflections.

Hold it! Click. Once more! And we smile again
at one who'll be irrevocably absent.
Quick. Be quick! the tulips, like swans, will dip
their heads deep into the polished table
frightening us. Thank you. And we turn thinking,

What a fuss! Yet decades later, dice thrown,
we'll hold it, thank you, this fable of gone
youth (was that us?) and we shall smile please
and come a little nearer to the impetuous
once-upon-a-time that can never be twice.

(Never never be twice!) Yet we'll always recall
how white tulips, quick quick, changed into swans
enthralled, drinking from a polished table.
As for those white petals, they'll never fall
in that little black coffin now carrying us.

Thomas Hardy

AFTER A JOURNEY

Hereto I come to view a voiceless ghost;
    Whither, O whither will its whim now draw me?
Up the cliff, down, till I'm lonely, lost,
    And the unseen waters' ejaculations awe me.
Where you will next be there's no knowing,
    Facing round about me everywhere,
      With your nut-coloured hair,
And gray eyes, and rose-flush coming and going.

Yes: I have re-entered your olden haunts at last;
    Through the years, through the dead scenes I have tracked you;
What have you now found to say of our past –
    Scanned across the dark space wherein I have lacked you?
Summer gave us sweets, but autumn wrought division?
    Things were not lastly as firstly well
      With us twain, you tell?
But all's closed now, despite Time's derision.

I see what you are doing: you are leading me on
    To the spots we knew when we haunted here together,
The waterfall, above which the mist-bow shone
    At the then fair hour in the then fair weather,
And the cave just under, with a voice still so hollow
    That it seems to call out to me from forty years ago,
      When you were all aglow,
And not the thin ghost that I now frailly follow!

Ignorant of what there is flitting here to see,
 The waked birds preen and the seals flop lazily;
Soon you will have, Dear, to vanish from me,
 For the stars close their shutters and the dawn whitens hazily.
Trust me, I mind not, though Life lours,
 The bringing me here; nay, bring me here again!
  I am just the same as when
Our days were a joy, and our paths through flowers.

Pentargan Bay

Acknowledgements

We are grateful to the poets and copyright-holders for permission to include the poems in this collection as follows. Where no source is given, the poem is previously unpublished in book form.

DANNIE ABSE: 'Photograph and White Tulips' from *Arcadia, One Mile*, Hutchinson, London, 1998. Copyright © Dannie Abse 1998. By permission of The Peters Fraser and Dunlop Group Limited.

FLEUR ADCOCK: 'For a Five-Year-Old'. Copyright © Fleur Adcock 1983. Reprinted from *Selected Poems*, 1983, by permission of Oxford University Press.

JOHN AGARD: 'How Laughter Made Clock Smile' from *Laughter is An Egg*, Puffin Books, 1991. Copyright © John Agard 1991. By permission of Caroline Sheldon Literary Agency.

MONIZA ALVI: 'My Father's Father's Father' from *A Bowl of Warm Air*, Oxford University Press, 1996. Copyright © Moniza Alvi 1996. By permission of Moniza Alvi.

ANONYMOUS INUIT: 'The Old Man's Song' from *Peter Freuchen's Book of the Eskimos*, edited by Dagmar Freuchen, Arthur Barker, London, 1962. Copyright © Peter Freuchen Estate 1961.

SIMON ARMITAGE: 'Two Clocks' copyright © Simon Armitage 1999. By permission of the author.

W. H. AUDEN: 'If I Could Tell You'. Copyright © 1945 by W. H. Auden. Reprinted by permission of Random House, Inc.. By permission of Faber and Faber, London and Curtis Brown Ltd.

FRANCES BELLERBY: 'Ends Meet' from *Selected Poems*, Enitharmon Press, London, 1970. Copyright © Frances Bellerby 1970. By permission of Charles Causley, Literary Executor.

OLIVER BERNARD: translation of 'Barbarian' from *Rimbaud: Selected Verse*, Penguin Books, London, 1962. Reprinted by permission of Penguin Books.

SUJATA BHATT: 'Sruti' from *The Stinking Rose*, Carcanet Press, Manchester, 1995. Copyright © Sujata Bhatt 1995. By permission of Carcanet Press.

Index of Poets

* indicates translator

Some Recent Poetry from Anvil

Heather Buck
Waiting for the Ferry

Nina Cassian
Take My Word for It

Peter Dale
Dante: The Divine Comedy
Edge to Edge
SELECTED POEMS

Dick Davis
Touchwood

Carol Ann Duffy
The World's Wife
LIMITED EDITION

Martina Evans
All Alcoholics Are Charmers

Nikolai Gumilyov
The Pillar of Fire
TRANSLATED BY RICHARD McKANE

Michael Hamburger
Collected Poems 1941–1994
Late

Donald Justice
Orpheus Hesitated Beside the Black River
NEW AND SELECTED POEMS 1952–1997

Marius Kociejowski
Music's Bride

Peter Levi
Reed Music

The publisher
would like to thank
the National Maritime Museum
in Greenwich
for its help in making
this book possible